Taylor Made:

Poetry, Prose, and Reflections

Taylor Made:

Poetry, Prose, and Reflections

Dr. Ray Noble Taylor

Dedication

To my wife, Frances,
and to my children,
Nicole and Ray, Jr.;
and to my grandchildren,
Ray III, Joseph, and Carter.
To my brothers and sister,
those with us and gone,
And their children.
To all the spouses,
to aunts and uncles,
to those present and those with
the Lord.
And to my parents—
Rev. Chester H. Taylor and
Floda Mae Taylor.

Acknowledgments

I began this book without having a clue as to what I was getting into. Rapidly, I found out why I had been procrastinating for forty-plus years. The task would have been impossible without the awesome skills and patience of my editor, and Sarasota, Florida's gift to the world, Liz Coursen. Her ability to reignite the passion for writing in an eccentric old man goes beyond any words in my vocabulary!

Kudos must also go out to a dear family friend, Celeste Betjemann. She not only was relentless in getting my wife and me to move to Florida, but was like a kind bulldog in destroying my excuses for not finishing "that book."

When it was suggested that I use a free-hand artist's depiction of an old photo on the front cover of my book, the expected choice was to use a seasoned professional artist. After one look, I said I need an artist who knows my spirit. I told my editor that I knew an artist who, as a child, had done a prize-winning free-hand drawing of me. My daughter, Nicole, who I call "first baby," blew my mind with her rendering of a picture of me in my late 20s, which now graces the cover of this book. Nicole continues to enrich my life.

Finally, my friend of over 40 years, whom I call "the fixer," is Dr. Randall Morgan. Randall is not only a great orthopedic surgeon, he is a great "anything-you-need" person. Wherever he lives, he inserts himself into the community, helping in any way he can. Whatever I needed as I learned my way around Sarasota, Florida, Randall was there to help. When I was told by my editor that I needed someone to write a Foreword, Randall was the obvious choice. His sincerity and literary expressions touched me deeply, just as I expected they would.

Dr. Ray N. Taylor,
March, 2019

Foreword

To read about the journey taken by one you highly respect is always an adventure and a treat.

Dr. Ray N. Taylor provides an honest, humorous, introspective and sometimes painful view of all the elements that it takes to become a man. His adventure places great emphasis on the impact of family on our lives when we are young and naïve, but even more when we are mature and seasoned.

There is a true description of the important men in Dr. Taylor's life, spanning four generations. Many men know very little about the men in their family, much to their detriment and to that of our society.

The strength of men, as depicted in many ways, is one of the important messages of this remarkable collection of poetry and prose. I marvel at how the poet can place sometimes simple words and sometimes less used but very descriptive words in just the correct order to challenge our thinking and our understanding.

Since I have been blessed to have relatives who are skilled at writing poetry and use it to express very sensitive moments and very powerful thoughts, I appreciate the importance of poetry in the life of Dr. Taylor. His alternating use of poetry and prose is a unique way to teach the lessons of life. He allows the reader to share some of his most intimate thoughts and emotions about the things that many of us feel but are hesitant to speak about.

Dr. Taylor and I grew up in the same city, Gary, Indiana, but viewed life through different lenses in some ways and through the same lens in many other ways. However, our journey brought us both back to serve those who were responsible for our growth and success in our hometown. It brought us back to serve under the tutelage and sometimes competition created by strong Black male fathers who migrated to the North to escape the racial oppression of Alabama and Mississippi respectively. Yet we are who we are because of them.

I enjoyed Dr. Taylor's appeal to honesty and his self-deprecation, which most of the time was not warranted! There is no better way for a successful person to inspire others than to be sensitive to the attributes of his fellow man. When I read his poems multiple times, I begin to understand the power of the poet to express power, perspective, respect, and love in ways that can influence and relate to each of our lives.

Randall C. Morgan Jr., MD, MBA
March 2019

Table of Contents

Introduction

Explanations before you judge... Muhammad Ali said (and I paraphrase): "If you are the same at 50 as you were at 20, then you have wasted 30 years." My language, over time, has been refined, not coarsened.

I say this to explain that there are words that I used freely in my 20s that I rarely use at the age of 79.

One specific word that can be used as a term of endearment or insult is the word "nigger." A common saying which I, and many black males in their 20s would say to each other was this: "You're my nigger if you don't get no bigger; and if you get bigger, you'll be my big nigger." Now, a white man, of any age, is not allowed to use this phrase; and I can't recall the last time I heard a mature black man use it!

Other words which I used more frequently in my youth were those of a profane nature. If we are honest, sometimes nothing expresses our feelings better than profanity. I'm a P.K. (preacher's kid) and I've heard heathens and devout folks, young and old, express themselves with pretty colorful language when pushed over the edge. I confess that even now, as I experience Florida drivers, my language encompasses the entire color spectrum. However, as I mature, the frequency of my outbursts is inverse to my age.

I do all this explaining to prevent the reader from being totally shocked at some of the words of a 79-year-old, retired military oral surgeon, who is also an ordained minister. Just remember that many of the words are descriptive observations. More importantly, remember that the writer's words are those of an untrained poet going through life's stages. God put those words in his head in an unfiltered manner. He was, at times, young and old, uneducated and educated, mad and glad, happy and sad, but, always growing. Always.

Now, before I proceed, I would like to introduce you to two sets of couples who were influential in my life. I only wrote poems about the men. This is probably because I can not possibly insert myself into the feelings of women.

The first couple is Zorah Sarah Cynthia Drusella Hall Prewitt and Will Henry Prewitt. They were my maternal grandparents. I remembered Grandma Zorah's entire name because I was astounded at its length and complexity. Those were not the only amazing things about her. She made the best breakfast biscuits (bar none) in the world and had the intuitive ability to talk to kids as co-equals. Her most incredible gift, however, was her tolerance for Will Henry Prewitt. They were together for well over 50 years. She must have loved him!

Will Henry Prewitt was a piece of work. He was a small, poorly educated man who could have passed for a poor white Alabama tenant farmer. Except for the "white" part, this assessment was accurate. One thing about him stood out: He absolutely lit up any room into which he came. After a couple drinks, his witticisms and aphorisms sprang forth! If he saw pretty ladies who looked playful, he would say: "Whenever you see me, you see Will and them." They would answer: "Them who, Papa Will?" "Them Dollars!" he would retort. To large men who didn't like his banter, he would give this sinister hint: "You never see Will alone. He always has his six brothers with him." Street folks knew the bulge beneath his jacket hid a Colt 45 six-shot pistol. Everybody laughed; nobody bothered him. Amazingly, he survived the "juke-joints" of rural Alabama and the inner cities of Gary and Chicago. In his old age, he stopped drinking, went to church every Sunday, and slept away life peacefully in my mother's upstairs bedroom.

Introduction

My next introduction is to Floda Mae Prewitt Taylor and Rev. Chester Howard Taylor, my mother and father. They grew up in farm country around Northport, Alabama. Floda Mae was the third of six daughters of Will and Zorah Prewitt. She was, also, one of the smartest and prettiest girls in their small, close-knit Alabama community. She was a "catch" and Chester knew it!

Chester was the "baby boy" of George and Bell Taylor's large family. While the Prewitts were tenant farmers, the Taylors owned their farm. Chester was the class "goof-off" in school and struggled to read. Since he always wanted to be a preacher, that was not good. The local pastors let him preach because he would listen and mimic others' sermons. At the ages of 16 and 18, Floda and Chester decided to marry. They moved into the large Taylor farmhouse with Chester's parents. Chester worked at several menial jobs in town and continued preaching when possible. In 1938, Chester Jr., came along. Ray Noble was born in 1940. Wanda Bruce joined the family in 1942 and the farmhouse was getting crowded! World War II had begun and Chester heard about good jobs in aircraft factories in Chicago. He migrated to Chicago and was hired. Of course, he had to join a church and found Calvary Temple Baptist. The pastor needed an assistant and Chester filled the void. Rev. R. E. Eddington was happy to mentor, license, and ordain the eager young preacher. He also told Chester to send for his family and provided them all space in his large home. In 1944, bouncing baby Billy joined the family and things got crowded again.

Then, God stepped in. A small church of 20 people in Gary needed a pastor. Rev. Chester H. Taylor preached a trial sermon for them and "blew their socks off" as one deacon described it. All the Deacon Board wanted to have a church vote, except one senior deacon. He believed Chester was lacking educationally. That senior deacon was voted down. The church voted overwhelmingly and Chester was a pastor. Later, that deacon became

Chester's strongest supporter and chairman of the Deacon Board. It was a good move. Rev. Chester H. Taylor grew that church from 20 to 1,000 members. The church built a beautiful parsonage for the family, who moved from Chicago to Gary in 1952. The new church building was completed in 1954 and we marched in singing "We're marching up to Zion, that beautiful city of God." About twenty years later, I wrote a poem about Rev. Chester H. Taylor called "The Dummy." Some "dummy," huh?

Finally, a little about me. I am the second of four children of Rev. Chester H. Taylor and Floda M. Taylor. We are truly children of the great migration, stimulated by the oppression of the descendants of slaves who dared to want to be truly free. My father refused to allow his children to be denied the dignity to which all human beings are entitled. Even though Chicago was not the panacea he dreamed about, at least there we had a chance.

I wish I could say that I always took advantage of the new opportunities available to me, but I did not. I always knew that I was smart, but I did nothing about it, initially. My father, who I believe had learning disabilities, worked his butt off and worked miracles. I screwed up in high school; fortunately, God held me back and I was too young to work at U.S. Steel. My blessed mother suggested that I try college, seriously. The light came on (an epiphany?) and suddenly I became a good college student. My fraternity, Kappa Alpha Psi, encouraged my scholastic abilities and my parents ensured that I had no financial difficulty. I was accepted into Indiana University School of Dentistry. I did well, but found I did not like general dentistry. Instead of dropping out, I consulted with my adviser, who suggested I try oral surgery. In the Army, I found that I was good at it. At Boston University School of Graduate Dentistry, I found out I was best in my oral surgery class. At Harlem Hospital I was elected Chief Resident and met the love of my life, Frances Joaquin. Frances grew up in a South Bronx project, and went on to become valedictorian of her nursing school class at Harlem Hospital and a graduate of Columbia University. After we married and moved back to Indiana, Frances became a vice president at our local hospital. Without God and my wife, I would be nothing.

Frequently, I am asked how I succeeded where so many of my race have failed. My answer is that I have not always succeeded and they have not always failed. When I was setting up my practice in Gary, I surveyed all the local black dentists and two white dentists who had always accepted black patients. I was told by two of the black senior dentists that a black oral surgeon should either teach at a dental school or go back into the military. I was promised patients by the two white dentists and one black dentist, who promised me *all* of his surgical patients. Those three dentists kept their promise. They saved my practice for my first four years. I can never repay them; my gratitude is eternal! My wife's success and the support of my father's church base ensured my financial security. This also allowed me to become the first (and I believe, the only) African-American oral surgeon to pass the certification examination of the American Board of Oral and Maxillofacial Surgery in the State of Indiana. Let me be clear: Jackie Robinson was the first black baseball player to play in Major League Baseball. He was not the *best*. He was the *best supported*. So was I! Case closed.

Sincerely, *Ray Noble Taylor*
March 2019

Prologue to "The Gentle Ones"

In order to explain the origin of this poem, we must take a journey back in time. If you asked a member of my 1957 high school graduation class at Gary Froebel High to describe me in two words, he or she would probably say, "extreme introvert." I barely spoke to people and was so shy that only a few friends and family knew that I stammered under stress. My wife of 48 years, Frances, who occasionally converses with former classmates of mine, is shocked at their remembrance of me. She tells them that I must be making up for lost time, because she cannot shut me up!

There must be reasons for this enigmatic disconnect between my former and present self. I will tell you what I believe and why writing entered into my life.

The first influence that I remember in my life is family. The Taylor family was a product of the great migration from the rural American South (Alabama) to the northern inner cities (in our case, Chicago). We were not educated middle class. We were "country" folks making it any way we could. Everyone knew their place. My father, who struggled with the books, somehow became a preacher. His wife, whom he married when she was sixteen, was called "Madear" by everybody. She was a stay-at-home mother who finished number one in her night school high school class. Chester Jr. was the oldest boy. He was not only born on Daddy's birthday but was the best athlete and best looking in the family. Wanda Bruce was the smartest, the slickest, and the only girl in the family. Billy was the baby boy and the most spoiled in the family. Me, I was just Ray. For some reason, the school system in Chicago gave me a "double promotion," allowing me to skip not one but two grades. Maybe it was because I was a natural speed reader. The only thing it did was put me in class with older students who treated me like a little brother. I felt like a social misfit and finished in the lower half of my inner city high school. There was one blessing: I was too young to work in the steel mills. There was an Indiana University Extension in Gary, and my mother made me register there. Amazingly, I became a good enough student to be accepted into Indiana University School of Dentistry and graduated in 1965!

Now, some folks may question and ask, what does all this stuff have to do with your writing poetry? Well, I am glad they asked. If they were paying attention, they would have noticed the many ups and downs in my story. Smarter people than I have described it as an example of the vicissitudes of life. A famous radio philosopher in the 1950s by the name of Paul Harvey always talked about telling "The rest of the story." Please allow me to do the same.

After registering at Indiana University Northwest in 1957, some amazing things happened to me. I, who had flunked algebra in a ghetto high school, got a "B" in trigonometry in college. I had to take it in order to take college chemistry, and I got a "B" in chemistry. When I went to I. U. Bloomington campus, I got an "A" in Spanish. I flunked Spanish in high school. In Bloomington, Kappa Alpha Psi, which was founded at I.U., took me as a member. Because of my grades, the fraternity members appointed me scholarship chairman. Then they discovered my singing gifts and appointed me songmaster of the fraternity. Then, things got really interesting: one of the duties of pledges was to write lyrics (a ditty) replacing those of popular songs, but relevant to our fraternity. I found that I could do it well. The lyrics replacing a Hebrew work song (Zum Gali)—which we called "Zoom Golly"—became nationally known in our fraternity. I never got credit for it officially, but I knew who wrote it.

When I graduated from dental school, I decided to serve two years in the U.S. Army Dental Corps. Subsequently, I did post-doctoral study at Boston University School of Graduate Dentistry in Oral Surgery before going to Harlem Hospital as Intern and Chief Resident in Oral Surgery. New York is where the rubber meets the road. To paraphrase Frank Sinatra: "If you can make it there, you'll make it anywhere." I wasn't sure I could.

This first formal attempt at poetry was written in 1968, as Halloween was approaching. To be honest, I was having a "pity party." I was a new intern in oral surgery at Harlem Hospital Center, and I felt overwhelmed and "country" in the big city. My peers were all aggressive "easterners," and I was a shy preacher's son from Gary, Indiana. The question in my mind was simple: "Can I hold my own?" My answer came in the form of this ode to self-assurance called "The Gentle Ones."

Taylor Made

The Gentle Ones

This cold cruel world, part trick, part
treat,
t'was not created for the sweet
The hard, the cruel, the strong go on,
the gentle wait for some sweet dawn.

They drown their pain in seas of hope,
The dimmest light and on they grope.
Searching for some good in man,
Reaching out with wounded hand.

Taylor Made

Offering their meager fruit,
Their faith, their love, their trust, their
truth.

And always there are those who take,
Their souls to rape and hearts to break.

But through their agonizing pain,
And hurt they feel, once more again.
They see a light and realize,
That light is brighter through the eyes
of one whose eye has held a tear,
for someone loved and someone dear.

So, maybe those who seem so weak,
With gentle ways and quiet mystique,
Are not the clowns we scorn with glee,
For we are blind and they can see.

Written by Ray Noble Taylor,
New York City, New York, October, 1968

Ray's family. Front row: The Rev. C. H.
Taylor and Floda Mae Taylor.
Back row, from left to right: Billy, Wanda
Bruce, Ray, and Chester.

Taylor Made

Prologue to "Will Henry"

"Will Henry" is the only poem I have written that consistently makes me cry. This is both irritating and cathartic to me. It is irritating because, as the song says, "A man ain't supposed to cry," and cathartic because it washes all my phony "macho" façade away.

Will Henry Prewitt was my grandfather on my mother's side. I believe he spent almost all his life, until the last few years, proving he could overcome overwhelming odds. It took a toll.

Will Henry was born in 1894, the second son of James and Melinda

Prewitt. "Grandpa Jim," as my mother called her grandfather James Prewitt, was a rare Negro in Samantha, Alabama, in those times. He was very literate and subscribed to the local newspaper, which he never failed to read. Even more amazingly, he was a landowner and farmed his own land. Unfortunately, Jim was not forewarned that if he did not pay property taxes for a certain time period, the person who paid the taxes could claim the land. White businessmen who knew the system and had access to tax records were quick to claim land from ignorant black landowners. Grandpa Jim and his sons—Cullen, Will, and Artie— wound up being tenant farmers on their own land.

Since courts never ruled in favor of Negroes over whites, Jim and his boys adapted to the system. They grew cotton and bartered with the new owners of their farm for minimal annual profit...if they were lucky. Vegetable gardens and livestock, supplemented with game they killed, fed the family.

Cullen and Will married two sisters—Hester and Zorah—and both started families. However, tragedy soon struck. One afternoon the brothers, who were both expert hunters, were out hunting rabbits. Will laid his gun against a tree and it fell on a rock, which caused it to fire, killing Cullen. I am sure Will was never the same person again. Hester never remarried.

Will and Zorah had six daughters. My mother, Floda Mae Prewitt Taylor, was the third born. In the agricultural south, Will and Zorah were unlucky. People had large families to work the fields; girls were not as strong as boys in the hot Alabama sun. Will Henry bowed his head and coped. Zorah and the girls did their best, but it was rough. Eventually, all the girls married and drifted north. The oldest, Toya, ended up in Chicago. Second and fourth oldest, Dimple and Juanita, moved with their husbands to Niagara Falls, New York. My mother, Floda, married Rev. C. H. Taylor and moved to Chicago also. She soon sent for her younger sisters, Doletha and Zonada, who lived with my family until they married Chicago men. My immediate family never lived alone until all the kids were grown; we always had relatives for company!

So, Will Henry and Mama Zorah were finally by themselves. It must have been difficult for Zorah. Will Henry, as you might imagine, had many issues. They soon manifested themselves in drinking, gambling, and a wandering eye. He also had the habit of saying exactly what was on his mind. In the south, this usually led to death or institutionalization for a black man. My parents would often send us to Alabama for the summer to get away from the temptations of Chicago's south side. I remember that Mama Zorah was manning the fort alone on our last visit. The older cousins told me that Papa Will was in the "crazy house." I think we all knew what that meant.

Soon thereafter, after we returned to Chicago, my mother told us that Mama Zorah was coming to live with us. That was fine; we were used to company and she was fun. After we moved to our new home in Gary, we were told that Papa Will

Henry was coming, too. We knew he was fun, also, but in a challenging way. Oh, what a wild ride we had with Will Henry in our teenage and young adult lives!

"Will Henry" needs more explanation than most poems. "Papa Will," or "Pops," was a character who, I later realized, had character. Contemporary peers would have a hard time understanding the travails of an undereducated, "white-looking Negro" in early twentieth century Alabama who had his inherited property stolen by a manipulative system. Overlay this with the fact that he had to be a tenant-farmer on this very land, and the insult is palpable.

The aforementioned situation contributed to dysfunctional personal and familial circumstances in Pops' life. As my immediate family moved north in the great migration, Papa Will Henry's penchant for appreciating the ladies as well as the local brewed "adult beverages," pushed my grandmother Mama Zorah to also move north. Anecdotally, Papa Will Henry's eccentricities (especially in the south) led to a brief stint in an institution. My parents sent for "Pops" and Will Henry and Zorah were re-united.

That's when the fun began. Papa Will Henry lied about his age and was hired as a USPS mail handler. In spite of his age, he worked so hard that younger men complained that he was making them look bad. He said mail bags were nothing compared to cotton bales. He continued to drink heavily on weekends, but, every Monday he was up drinking coffee at 5 AM and still out-working everyone at USPS.

He drove my preacher father and my saintly mother nuts, but my older brother Chester and I made sure we took care of him on his weekend jaunts to Chicago's West Side. Papa Will Henry was a "stitch" and took no "stuff" from my mischievous, chunky, baby brother Billy ("Bill the Hill") or my pugnacious, talkative sister, Wanda Bruce.

He liked women in more ways than one, but, respected their femininity and would have been horrified at the common domestic violence we see these days.

Prologue to "Will Henry"

I didn't really appreciate the subtle life lessons Papa Will Henry was teaching until he was gone.

Taylor Made

Will Henry

They say Will Henry was his name, and
booze and ladies was his game; but then
they say a "lotta thangs" that just ain't
true

For while he had a lightning eye, for
shapely breast and rounded thigh; there
were somethings Will Henry wouldn't
do

And while a few may laugh at this, and
hunch your friends and wink at "sis";

Taylor Made

if I think real hard, I'll think of one or
two

No matter, we'll get back to that, after
one or two lies and a little chat; so let's
just talk about this little man

Some say he was born in '94, with eyes
blue-gray like rifle bore; for many years
he lived from hand to hand

He stood no more than five-foot three,
and many only saw the glee; although
he slaved to work the white man's land

His arms were wiry, his back was strong,
and though he labored hard and long;
it's hard when they won't let you be a
man

And so he drank a bit too much, and
gambled some and wenched and such;
and Mama Zorah soon grew tired and
flat

Will Henry

So then she went up North to stay, and
some say they put "Pops" away; but I
don't put too darn much truck in that

Then younger days were full of thrills
with Papa chasing "Bill the Hill," and
catching him because he was so fat

Then roaring loud at Wanda Bruce,
and snaring Chester in his noose; to
make him drive him to some West Side
flat

And there he'd gamble and he'd drink,
and later on the pee would stink; for at
his age who'd think of things like that

Then home to the basement we would
sneak, and try to keep his roar a squeak;
but "Pops" would talk so loud he'd
shake the house

And then the Reverend would appear,
and to the corners we would tear; while
"Pops" sat at the table quiet as a mouse

Taylor Made

Now some might ask, what did he
teach, this little man with ruddy cheeks;
what did he leave to help you fight the
world?

My answer is he made the fight, with
crudest tools and all his might; through
all the rivers, whirlpools and the swirls

His education stopped grade three, but
newspapers he'd read daily; with
reading glasses struggling aloud

How many of us younger folks, who
used to laugh at him and joke, could
fight his battles and survive as proud

And those who always said he drank,
and wet his pants and made them
"stank"; do not recall he never missed a
day

For those short-changed on things like
school, because they had to guide that

mule, would rather toss mailbags all day
than hay

And debts were things you always paid,
if not they simply were not made; those
were the things that little old man
taught me

And women were not made to hit, and
men who did were less than shit; and
you just didn't do it around Will Henry

Now, one day soon my progeny will ask
what Papa meant to me; and I will dig
until I find this tome

I'll say grandson, he gave me fire, I
hope I will one day inspire, in you the
grace to someday write a poem.

Taylor Made

The Prewitt family, on Zorah and Will
Henry's 50th anniversary, circa 1955.
Front row: Mama Zorah and Will Henry.
Back row, left to right: Zonada, Doletha,
Juanita, Ray's mother Floda Mae, Dimple,
Toya.

Taylor Made

Prologue to "The Dummy"

"The Dummy" was written because I was mad! Notice, I did not say that I was angry or irritated. I was "p.o.'d." If someone said, "Shame, shame preacher," I would say that means "pretty offended." If I were a bit more "thuggish" or a better fighter, I would have punched someone in the nose. However, since I was a slight 150-pound doctor who couldn't "bust a grape with a hammer," I thought the better of it.

Why was I so upset? Well, I'm glad you asked—if you give me a minute, I'll tell you about it. I had decided to set up my oral surgery practice in Gary, Indiana, for two reasons. Initially, I thought the city, which had a thriving steel industry and a majority black population, needed me. The white oral surgery group was joining the "white flight" crowd. My second thought was that my father, who had given his life to his God through church ministry in our hometown, needed me as he aged. I had been out of town for over a decade as I completed my surgical training. Subsequently, I believed that since my father had taken a "basement church" of twenty-plus members in 1946 and grown it to almost a thousand in 1960, he would be respected. I am sure that most readers can understand my shock when my older brother came by my office and told me an unbelievable story in the year 1970.

He said, "Ray, I almost hit a nigger today!" With my eyes bugging out of my head, I took him back to my private office for a more detailed conversation. He told me a story that must have been growing while I was out of town. As it unraveled in its complexity, a few beams of light began to shine through. To make a long story short, acquaintances began to tease Chester about the nicknames of local preachers. My father was known as "the Dummy." Wow! I wanted to hit a nigger, too. But, I wasn't as good a fighter as Chester, and he couldn't whip the whole world, either. So, I told him that I had started writing again and would come up with something to calm us down.

I began looking back to my remembrances. Several truths and questions popped up in my mind. How did a "dummy" grow a church like Daddy had done? I noticed that he did well when speaking from memory, but was terrible when he had to read! Another reality popped into my head: because the literacy rate was so low in our working-class church, few people criticized Daddy's reading struggles. Then, I remembered an occasion when a former classmate asked me a strange question a few years back. He said, "How can your father be a pastor when he is in night school studying for a high school diploma?" I blew him off because the question made no sense to me. Suddenly, it hit me. Daddy wasn't happy with his status; he tried to change it. It didn't work; the word got out. They called him "dummy."

So, my next question was; what do I do about it? I didn't know anything about learning disabilities in 1970, but I knew one thing: I know a stupid person when I see one and my father was not stupid. My brother, Chester, was waiting for the writing promised to him and I wanted understanding for my dad. I racked my brain for anecdotes both ancient and more recent that I had heard over the years. Pictures began to form and rhyme and rhythm intertwined. Finally, logic and understanding began to be compatible. Questions began to arise. How many people who can't read get by on memory? Why do most of the churches with less educated members have choirs that use no music? They say Daddy was always the person clowning and cutting up both in school and in ministerial meetings and such. How many folks get by on charm? I began to see, also, that folks with a strong moral code and a tough demeanor are rarely challenged if they don't want to do mundane things like reading. Let somebody else do it; leave me alone. I knew what I had to do. Explain a person without disparaging him; highlight his strengths without condescension about his weaknesses.

"The Dummy" seems, initially, like a poem that insults. When I first presented it at an annual office anniversary celebration, I wasn't sure my Daddy would understand my counterpoint to his detractors. Black ministers are frequently misunderstood, especially by other men. Therefore, since they see these servants as predators, no insult is too harsh. In the pool halls and "juke-joints" around Lake County, in Gary, every prominent black preacher had a nickname: there was "The Hustler," "The Crook," "The Playboy," and Rev. C. H. Taylor, my daddy, was "The Dummy."

Actually, it's easy to understand the adversaries' confusion. Daddy never wanted to be anything but a preacher. As a pre-school kid, he could mimic any preacher he heard. He could listen and memorize sermons and whole chapters of the Bible, especially Psalms. There was only one problem: words on a page looked jumbled and confusing. Daddy disliked school and never finished. We would know how to teach him now. We would even have a word for his problem that they didn't have in the 1930s: dyslexia.

Daddy had another characteristic that all Taylors have. It is both a blessing and a curse; it is eccentricity. We are all energetic, personable, over-confident doers. As a little boy, Daddy would preach on the farm to chickens, dogs, horses—anything—and, they would listen! So, it should not surprise anyone that when the kind Pastor of Calvary Temple Baptist Church in Chicago, Rev. R. E. Eddington, mentored this uneducated country boy and practiced with him using the spoken word, Rev. Eddington found a charismatic preacher!

When Christian Valley M.B. Church in Gary needed a pastor for its "basement church," the dynamic young preacher who struggled to read grew it into one of the largest congregations in the city. He also sent two kids through college and one became a "speed reader" and a doctor.

My older brother wanted to fight about Daddy's insulting nickname; his younger brother wanted to write about it, so here you have it: "The Dummy."

Taylor Made

The Dummy

They say he was born down 'Bama way,
now when it was, I will not say

But he won't drink no gin or rummy,
and this is why some call him dummy.

The trees and stumps and cane and
sticks,
were things that made his first pulpit.

And members of the animal nation,
comprised his boyhood congregation.

Taylor Made

For he would preach to anything,
his voice would bellow, roar, and sing.

Eyebrows would raise and shoulders
hunch,
when he was preaching to those stumps.

His mother'd watch him and she'd
pray,
and all the others, they'd just say

Either he's drinking gin or rummy,
or else that boy is just a dummy.

He never cared that much for school,
just teasing, clowning, playing the fool.

Reminds me of another boy,
who got his own peculiar joy.

Confusing Elders by a sea,
I think they called it Galilee.

The Dummy

He never heard of gin or rummy,
but I'll betcha some called Him a
dummy.

And then he married Floda Mae,
and migrated up Chicago way.

Taking along their brood of three,
and even adding baby Billy.

The world was rumbling loud with war,
his dream was very much afar.

While scientists worked on nuclear
fission,
his mind conceived a peaceful vision.

"A church," he thought, "we must have
one,
and worship right the Master's Son."

And Reverend Eddington let him
preach,
in Sunday school he learned to teach.

Taylor Made

Then from a Gary church a call,
no fancier than that Bethlehem stall.

He made it worth a lot of bucks,
the other preachers called it luck.

"This man don't take no gin or rummy,
You know he's got to be a dummy.

He's never slept with others' wives,
rejects the politicians' bribes.

He never wants to have no fun,
he tells the truth on everyone.

He won't even steal a little bit,
he really believes that preacher shit.

Why everyone takes a little rummy,
That Taylor's got to be a dummy."

Yes, Daddy's like an open book,
in another man's kitchen, he won't
cook.

The Dummy

'Cause he doesn't know what's in the
pot,
he still believes that Hell is hot.

He placed those values in his son,
and those same obstacles I have run.

For when I wouldn't cheat in school,
I heard the epithet, "You Fool,"

"You pay all taxes without fail?"
My friends ask me, forgetting jail.

"Your Uncle Sam will never check,"
and next thing you know, your life's a
wreck.

But, I don't claim to be like Dad,
and in a way, I'm sort of glad.

If I could be a duplication,
Where would I get my inspiration?

Taylor Made

From Mother Dear I've oft been told,
When Dad was born they broke the
mold.

For once in life, that's not quite true,
God found some pieces He could glue.

I guess that makes me half the man,
and on that rock I'll proudly stand.

You see, I'll take a little rummy,
I'm glad that makes me half a dummy.

Written by Ray Noble Taylor,
Gary, Indiana, October, 1975

The Rev. C. H. Taylor at Chistian Valley
M.B. Church in Gary, Indiana, where he
was senior pastor for 58 years.

Taylor Made

Prologue to "The Help"

When I was two years old, my mother told me that my father decided to move our family from Samantha, Alabama, to the south side of Chicago. This emigration was a part of what historians call "The Great Migration."

Our departure was made for both social and economic reasons. We were second-class citizens because we were both black and poor. My father was an aspiring minister at that time, and his situation must have been especially painful. He was subjected to hearing racist white clergy quote the Bible in justifying the "Jim Crow" laws of the South. They used Genesis 9:25, which said Canaan shall be cursed to be a servant to his brothers. The white oppressors used the illiteracy of blacks against them. Blacks did not dig far enough into the biblical ancestry. If they had, they would have realized Noah had three sons: Shem, Ham, and Japheth. Traditionally, Biblical genealogists believe Shem begat Semitic peoples (Jews and others); Ham begat darker races (North- and sub-Saharan Africans); and Japheth begat fair-skinned races (whites and others). Ham's sons were Cush (black African), Mizraim (probably Egyptian), Put (probably Libyan), and Canaan (probably Palestinian). I don't believe in permanent generational curses. I believe white slave owners "cherry-picked" the Bible to explain their horrible behavior.

In spite of my father's irritation about white clergy, he became a successful, well-off minister, eventually founding a large church in Gary, Indiana. He raised his family to believe in strict Biblical doctrine. All the kids went through youthful rebellion, but I came back most fully. I was the child who truly believed Psalms 41:1: "Blessed is he that considereth the poor: the Lord will deliver him in time of trouble." I am the guy who sneaks that dollar to the panhandler at the intersection so my friends and family won't tell me how stupid I am. I don't care if he buys wine; a dollar won't hurt me and his children really might be hungry. Go ahead, laugh; I don't care! Full disclosure: I over-tip servers in restaurants unless they are really bad; I try to make up for cheap owners.

So, nobody who knows me should be surprised that I wrote a poem called "The Help." What's surprising is not that I wrote it, it's *when* I wrote it. Most avid readers know that the book of the same title came out in 2009. The superb movie with the same name was released in 2011. God directed me to write my poem in 1977. Go figure, I won't; I don't even try to read God's mind.

Some might ask: what was the prodding, the stimulus? Well, I must confess something. I, like most doctors, want to be great. But I, like most people, don't forget what Jesus said in both Matthew's and Mark's gospels: "Ye know that the princes of the Gentiles exercise dominion over them, and they that are great exercise authority upon them. But it shall not be so among you: but whosoever will be great among you, let him be your minister; and whosoever will be chief among you let him be your servant."

Wow! It really hit me. We, in dentistry and medicine are really servants. We are a *service* occupation! I noticed how arrogant I was as I trained my staff. *They are so ignorant compared to me*, I thought. Then I noticed how they looked down on poor, ignorant patients in pain as soon as they gained a little knowledge. Stop it! I said. We were all like that, not long ago.

I began to notice some doctors in the operating room and on the wards. They talked to nurses and technicians as though they were children. These were the people who helped to ensure smooth surgeries and calmed their patients through the night. How ungracious, such ingratitude. What would we do without them? They were our watchmen under hot lights and our angels through the night. Is it any wonder that nurses are our most respected professionals in every poll? Without the janitors, housekeepers, dietary workers, technicians, nurses, and, oh yes, doctors, our hospitals would collapse.

This poem, which was written in 1977, now seems almost prescient. I was a young surgeon who was very observant and I noticed how mean and condescending some doctors were to the people who assisted. After giving the matter some thought, I realized that I was not totally innocent. I knew that although I wasn't the worst, I could be kinder and more considerate.

Let's all give a big "shout out" to all the servants in the world, including ourselves.

So, yes; I confess that I wrote in anger. But, the writing assuaged the anger and I found the soothing tonic that

is found in the Prologue to "The Help."
One word: *respect.*

The Help

There is a small selective group, distinguished by perennial youth; and we all call this special troop, "The Help."

We never notice when they're there, but absence makes us stomp and swear; and just like some old ugly bear, we yelp.

Our ways make them competitive, we demand work that's substantive; yet when they show initiative, we squelch.

Taylor Made

We get them with their youthful curls,
and quickly put gray in those swirls;
but, to us they stay boys and girls, that's
cool.

We choose them 'cause they're rather
bright, our teaching methods are "out-a-
sight"; but despite all these things so
right, they're fools.

We rarely praise jobs done ably, "Why,
I could teach a bright monkey"; and we
usurp their skills with glee, that's cruel.

So we change a bright kid to a fool, who
never grows up and has no tools; now
who's the dummy in this school. You,
fool.

O.K., I think we've made our point,
about those guys who self-anoint; and
keep their noses out of joint. "Hi, Doc."

The Help

With just a few exaggerations, we've all come to our proper stations; we're merely service occupations, we can't stop.

Just as the waiter who serves the tea, we must dispense some sympathy; for without some humility, we flop.

Poor folks bring pain and ignorance; if we don't bring some common sense, instead of all this arrogance, we're dropped.

You see, it wasn't long ago; this fancy stuff we didn't know, and people called us worse things than "The Help."

Then future doctors went to college; got self-possessed with all that knowledge, and with the slightest ego bruise, we yelp.

Taylor Made

We trained our staffs via education; they took this as an elevation, above that lowly designation, called "Help."

Hey, let's stop all this fast ascension and all that phony condescension; let's plant our feet just once more on the ground.

We're here to serve those who're afraid, and understand their sad tirades; for though we're up, one day we may be down.

And all we've learned will be for naught, and we'll just have one plaintive thought, "Dear God, I 'sho' do hope **The Help** is around."

Ray Taylor with Rosa Rodriguez, his office
supervisor, Spanish interpreter, and
emergency surgical tech, in 1976.

Taylor Made

Prologue to "The Loser"

When I wrote this poem called "The Loser," several of my friends said, "Why in the hell would you write a poem about a loser?" Initially, I replied, "Because he's not." Then, after some reflection, I figured out that he wasn't really a loser, but he was *this* time. I really didn't know what type of poem it was, let alone what it really meant, until I quoted it to one of my best friends who was a third-generation black physician (I was a first-generation college graduate). He said, "Ray, that's whimsy." I pretended to know what "whimsy" meant, and secretly looked it up that night. Essentially, "whimsy" is something silly or odd, ending with an unexpected result. I said to myself, "Yeah, that's my poem, alright!"

But, the aforementioned statement doesn't really tell readers why I wrote the poem, does it? All right, I'll try to explain. As a young black male growing up in the inner city and just post-pubescent, one of our over-arching goals was to be a "dude" who "had it going on." In the 1950s, that meant you had somewhat "good hair" (not too nappy), nice rags (clothes), and could talk the talk (rap) and walk the walk (you had swag before you knew what it was). If you had any kind of car in our urban school, you had friends (both female and male) you didn't even know existed!

My father (God bless him in Heaven) made two big mistakes when his kids were at Gary Froebel High School in the 1950s. His namesake, Chester, Jr., was an import from Burnside Elementary school on the south side of Chicago. The rest of our family had moved into the new church parsonage in Gary, but Chester had begged to graduate with his friends from eighth grade in Chicago. He was allowed to stay with my mother's sister, Zonada, until this occurred. When he entered Froebel as a freshman in 1953, he was an immediate sensation! The boys liked him, because his teams usually won in intramural sports. He was also glib, quick with a joke, and laughed with you, not at you. And the girls? All they could say was, "Lord, have mercy." Curly black hair, large brown "doe-like eyes"; neither the girls nor competing fellows had a chance!

Then, my father made his first mistake. In Chester's sophomore year at Froebel High, Daddy said he was tired of leaving his pastoral duties to drive us kids all around. Chester had gotten his driver's license and a job in a carwash the previous summer. Dad said if he saved his money from his summer job for gas, etc., he would buy him a used car. Well, that old 1948 red Ford convertible was a canvas to paint on for Chester. Boy, was he creative with cars. By the time school started, that old Ford had a new paint job, imitation whitewall tires and imitation fur seats, back *and* front. That car was the hit of Froebel. It was always packed with guys (who would pitch in for gas) or girls (I won't tell you what they contributed) until the summer of 1954. We had discovered pretty girls lived in East Chicago, Indiana, also. One night, a group of us Gary guys were visiting an East Chicago girl's house when the word got out to jealous guys in the neighborhood. When we were ready to leave, we beheld a horrible sight: that cute little Ford had both its top and all four tires cut to ribbons. Our Dad banned us from East Chicago, took the insurance payment, and told Chester he would decide what to do in September, when school started.

That's when Daddy made his second huge mistake. He asked Chester if he had saved in the summertime. He said if he had, he wanted to take him somewhere. "Somewhere" turned out to be Shaver Chevrolet Motors on Broadway in Gary. Chester drove home in a brand new 1955 yellow Chevy 210 2-door hardtop. That was it! Studies were out, swag was in.

Chester was the uncrowned King of Froebel. I was just his little brother, but, there were fringe benefits. Many of his beautiful girl friends had beautiful friends or cute little sisters. I wasn't as cute; however, I was all right and I did all right. What wasn't right was my academics. I didn't tell Chester that he was my hero and role model, though most people probably knew. If he didn't care about school, I didn't either. If you had asked most young black men in my era if being a "player" was a primary goal in life, they would have said, "Oh, *yeah*." Fortunately, God and my blessed Mother re-directed me. But we still have memories, don't we?

It's amazing how many people still remember my swashbuckling brother (who is now 80 years old and still handsome) and shy little me (who is still secretly shy and still all right). I think that in their heart of hearts many black men wish they could have been a "player" like Chester. My problem was, and still is, that I do not multi-task well. So, as I sat around chewing the fat with a senior pastor who knew my brother well, he asked me a poignant question which I answered honestly. He said, "Ray, tell me the truth. Were you a player like your brother Chester?" I said, "Pastor, there's one difference. Chester was a player. I was a player wanna-be."

Now, in my reflective maturity, I often wonder who are the real winners and losers in life. I have met a few guys like my brother Chester and many guys like myself. Recently, I found a medallion online with an inscription so true that I sent it to my son. It said: "Life is not about winning and losing, it's about winning and learning."

Almost everyone knows someone like "The Loser." We're all a little jealous of him (if we are honest). They are almost too good looking to be a man. They're not particularly nice to women, but it doesn't seem to matter. The girls eat them up!

I have a brother like that, so everybody assumes that this poem is about Chester. No. Then they say, "It must be about you." No; I'm not nearly good-looking enough.

Prologue to "The Loser"

He's really a compilation of many "guys like that." We are all winners and losers, sometimes.

So as you read the poem, I think you'll recognize some "guys like that."

Taylor Made

The Loser

He walks with cool and somewhat
haughty air,
and unabashedly they stare

"My Lord for him I think I'd be a
sinner."
It's obvious that he's a winner

His hair is black and afro long;
his skin a shade of reddish-bronze

Taylor Made

The nose is straight and aquiline,
and chippies say "Ooh! That nigger's
fine."

His eyes are bright and "kinda" twinkle;
made mischievous by lines that "kinda"
crinkle

The world's his onion, so they say;
he "kinda" thinks that it should be that
way.

And then one day she came along,
and quickly changed our hero's song.

Her hair was soft and fresh as "chickee
down";
the skin a warm and toasty golden
brown.

With breasts so ripe and waist so very
small;
you know that nigger had to fall.

The Loser

"I've heard your line and somewhat
more,
from dudes who really know the score.

And all that witty rap and other things,
has such an old and tired familiar ring.

And all your deep and smooth
profundity,
don't really mean a doggone thing to
me.

And deeper minds than yours, I've
often blown,
so you can keep on keeping on."

So then a quick and very witty friend,
perceived in him what happens to all
men.

"Say, 'bro,' you're awfully quiet today,
and that is not your natural swinging
way.

And what's that in your eye, some
mist?"
"Naw, man, I'm really feeling rather
sick.

In fact, I haven't been too well
But, anyway, you go to hell."

Then silently he stole away,
to live to fight another day.

And to his secret heart, confess,
"She got me, but I'll be alright....I
guess."

The Taylor brothers, circa 1980, at their
parents' vacation home in Northport,
Alabama. From left to right:
Chester, Billy, and Ray.

Taylor Made

Prologue to "To Love"

Love is a complex, often irrational element in the life of most people. I remember hearing a sarcastic wit, early in my young adult life say: "Love is blind. Never fall in love, because that would be like the blind leading the blind." That is weird, but, somewhat truthful.

My first exposure to the concept of love came from my religious parents. Studying the Bible was not an option in the lives of the Taylor children. I learned very early in life that my mother's favorite Bible verse was 1 John 4:8: "He that loveth not knoweth not God; for God is love." Now, don't get that twisted. My parents weren't dishing out mushy, "kissy-face" love. That came with the grandkids. We didn't get "I love you, have a good night's sleep" before bed. It was more like "Get in that bed; you all have school in the morning." Tough love was the name, obedience was the game. Affection had to come from other sources. My parents raised four kids in the inner city of Gary, Indiana. It was a tough job; they were up to the task.

Let me say a few things about love before we go too deeply into this discussion. The Greeks thought so much about love that they had four different words for it.

The first word is *eros*. This is the love that husbands and wives feel for each other; but, also, the one that first makes boys and girls feel an unfamiliar titillation that makes them blush and stammer. It's called sexual love; enough said.

The second word is *phileo*. We recognize it in Philadelphia, the city of brotherly love. It's about friendship. Couples reach it if their relationship truly matures; boys and girls do not if they never grow up.

The third word is *stergo*: family love. If couples stay together and have children, they become parents. This is where the "blood is thicker than water" love comes into being.

Finally, we get to the fourth word. It is the greatest love of all (sorry Whitney Houston and Muhammad Ali). It is *agape*. It is self-sacrificing love best represented by Jesus Christ, who made the ultimate sacrifice. We know we have it for someone if it is totally unconditional. It is a "no matter what" love. It is extremely rare.

But, the question asked in this Prologue is, why did I write "To Love"? I believe the answer is both simple and complicated. I looked back over my shoulder and saw the love story of my life. It was both silly and serious. Looking back to my high school years, I remember two sisters. They were both beautiful. One was silly and one was serious. I became enchanted by the serious one. When I expressed my interest, she did not reciprocate. Why do we most desire that which we cannot have? I pressed her relentlessly; she finally consented to go with me to the spring affair called the "May Dance." Retrospectively, I believe pity was her reason. I now know why I love my favorite song by Bonnie Raitt. It's a reality check with a line that goes: "I can't make you love me, if you don't." Subsequently, two serious and silly things happened which related to this interlude in my life. I kept the "May Dance" photograph among my belongings. My wife came upon it one day. She inquired about it. I told her, "Oh, that's a picture of my high school crush. Don't worry; it was strictly a one-way deal. She's M.W.R., a sorority sister of yours." She laughed and acknowledged knowing her. We're all good friends. A funnier story involved my daughter. She is very protective of her mother. When she was about nine years old, she, also, came upon the infamous "May Dance" photo. Instantly recognizing me at the age of 15, she said, "Daddy, who is that girl with you?" I quickly told her that she was a girl I knew long before I knew her mother! Finishing up my explanation, I said, "Don't worry, she didn't like me very much." She gave me a quizzical look and went and told her mother, who got a good laugh!

After surviving my first devastating crush, I confess to many more on the road to maturity. There were some wins and some losses, but they were all building blocks in becoming the guy who can really appreciate the blessings of real love. Many people have asked why I wanted to look back on the pain and pleasure of this life experience. It's because it made me who I am.

My wife is still (almost 40 years later) trying to figure out about whom I am writing. Well, the answer is almost everybody I ever had a crush on. The range goes from the silly "puppy love" dramas where the little girls thought I was a stalker to my final, silly, "eternal love," which, of course, is my dear Frances L.J. Taylor.

So there; I love you and there is nothing you can do about it! Step into love.

To Love

To love is to be **honest**; to let the truth escape even if it damages your love, and threatens to destroy your love. A lie is sometimes permissible as a temporary measure; to protect a dear one from hurt which is so severe that it may be crushing. But eventually, perhaps tempered by time, the truth must always exit; for nothing kills love more quickly than deception.

To love is to be **helpless** at times. In spite of constant rebuffs and the more damaging defeat of unconcern, true love is not so easily driven away. It faces these twin onslaughts almost masochistically and returns ever stronger. Such is the helplessness of a love so true.

To love is to even be rendered **hopeless** on occasion; to become a quivering mass of defeatism. Life, as you now live it, temporarily appears to not be worth it all. Tears come hotly, quickly, uncontrollably. The sweet spring morning brings no hope; the crisp fall afternoon brings no relief; the aroma of hot bread in a familiar kitchen does not strike the usual warm satisfactory chord. All the little things which give us the will to exist are rendered meaningless. Such is the misery of the hopelessness of love.

To love is **Heaven** when it is good. Can Heaven be any more beautiful than her soft wakening touch in the morning;

her kiss hot with passion or cooling and soothing when all passion is spent; or simply a look so full of adoration when only a look is possible? Oh yes! Love is so much like Heaven when it is good.

To love is **Hell** when it is bad. Can anything be more hellish than unreciprocated love or pettiness in love. To merely want to be around and be punished with flight; to simply want to look in eyes which are content with aversion; oh, such agony! To be wrong, so wrong and try to wait for her to say "I'm sorry" with the near certainty that it will not come...this time. Hell is seemingly a better place than unrequited love.

But, to love is always to **hope.** When all seems over and irretrievable, she is suddenly, unexpectedly around. You search for anything: an innocent smile or act of kindness and your heart is racing; a touch is more precious than a crown jewel; a familiar gesture or nuance and you say, "Ah, I have it—a chance." Such is the tiny spark that always resides in the heart of one who loves.

So love, essentially, is a selfless thing. It is easy to have qualities which make you lovable. No effort is required from those who are given love; who suck its sweet juices until it is dry and withers and dies. The true lover is one who takes that largest of risks: to expose all tender and vulnerable places of himself. He is a giver who, at times, is made honest, helpless, hopeless; to be in Heaven or Hell, but always hopeful. He is not always seen with palms upward, expectant. He (or she) is that person seen with hands full; offering that most precious gift: the ability **To Love.**

The Rev. C. H. Taylor and Floda Mae
Taylor on their seventieth wedding
anniversary, December 31, 2006.

Taylor Made

Dr. Ray Taylor is available for poetry readings and workshops.

A discount is offered for bulk orders of 20 or more copies of *Taylor Made.*

Dr. Taylor can be contacted at rayraysr1940@gmail.com.

58523215R00059

Made in the USA
Columbia, SC
22 May 2019